CONTENTS

Squid 6

Glow-worm 8

Deep-sea dragonfish 10

Atolla jellyfish 12

Anglerfish 15

Firefly 16

Red tide 19

Click beetle 20

Venus flytrap anemone 22

Midwater jellyfish 25

South American polka dot tree frog 26

Shortnose greeneye fish 29

Glossary 30

Books 31

Websites 31

Comprehension questions 32

Index 32

Look at those glowing lights in the ocean! Did you know that some animals make their own light? When an animal gives off its own light, it's called bioluminescence. Sometimes it's called "cold light". The light doesn't make any heat. Many bioluminescent animals are found in the oceans. In fact, bioluminescence probably started in sea animals.

Magical An
Give Off Li

by Nikki Potts

Raintree is an imprint of Capstone Global Library Limited, a company incorporated in England and Wales having its registered office at 264 Banbury Road, Oxford, OX2 7DY – Registered company number: 6695582

www.raintree.co.uk
myorders@raintree.co.uk

Edited by Jaclyn Jaycox
Designed by Ashlee Suker
Picture research by Tracy Cummins
Production by Tori Abraham
Originated by Capstone Global Library Ltd
Printed and bound in India

ISBN 978 1 4747 5164 3 (hardback)
21 20 19 18 17
10 9 8 7 6 5 4 3 2 1

ISBN 978 1 4747 5168 1 (paperback)
22 21 20 19
10 9 8 7 6 5 4 3 2 1

British Library Cataloguing in Publication Data
A full catalogue record for this book is available from the British Library.

Acknowledgements
We would like to thank the following for permission to reproduce photographs: Alamy: Bluegreen Pictures/David Shale, 14, Brandon Cole Marine Photography, 7, Doug Perrine, 15, Jim Cole, 24, Nature Picture Library/Kim Taylor, 21; Getty Images: Alexander S. Kunz, 4-5, 18, Universal History Archive/UIG, 23; Minden Pictures: David Shale, 10, 11, 25, Pete Oxford, 27, Solvin Zankl, Cover; Newscom: Splash, 13; NOAA: 22; SeaPics.com: Michael Aw, 12; Shutterstock: Alexey Stiop, Cover Back, 2, Cathy Keifer, 17, Dr Morley Read, 20, Gallinago_media, 8, Ioana Filipas, 19, Jes2u.photo, 16, littlesam, 1, Martin Prochazkacz, 9, Patrick K. Campbell, 26, Tracey Winholt, 6; Wikimedia: NOAA, 28, NOAA OKEANOS Explorer Program, 2013 Northeast U. S. Canyons Expedition, 29

We would like to thank Jody Rake, Southwest Marine Educators Association, for her invaluable help in the preparation of this book.

SQUID

Squid swim in both deep and shallow areas of the ocean. Many types of squid give off blue or green light. They use their light to protect themselves from predators. The light from the squid blends in with sunlight shining into the ocean waters. This makes it hard for predators to see their prey, and keeps the squid safe from attack!

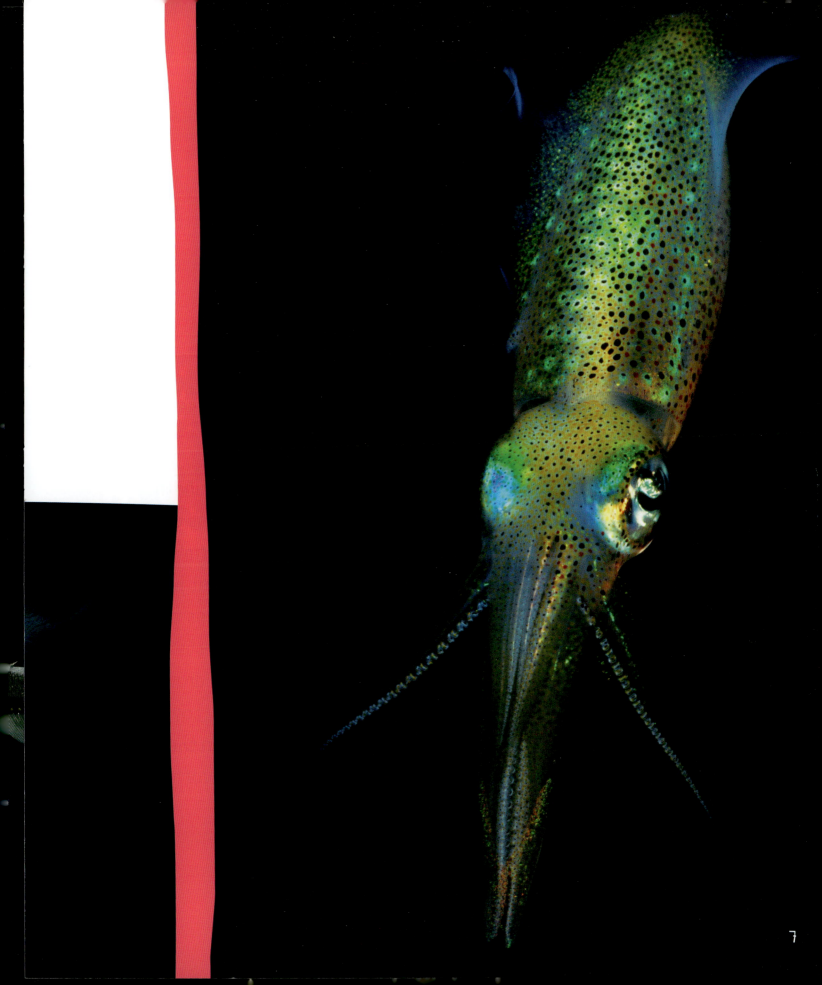

ATOLLA JELLYFISH

The Atolla jellyfish lives in the "midnight zone". This ocean zone is between 1,000 and 4,000 metres (3,280 and 13,123 feet). When scared by a predator, an Atolla jellyfish turns on blue lights. The lights encircle its body. Some people think the lights attract an even larger predator. A larger predator may distract the first predator, allowing the jellyfish to escape.

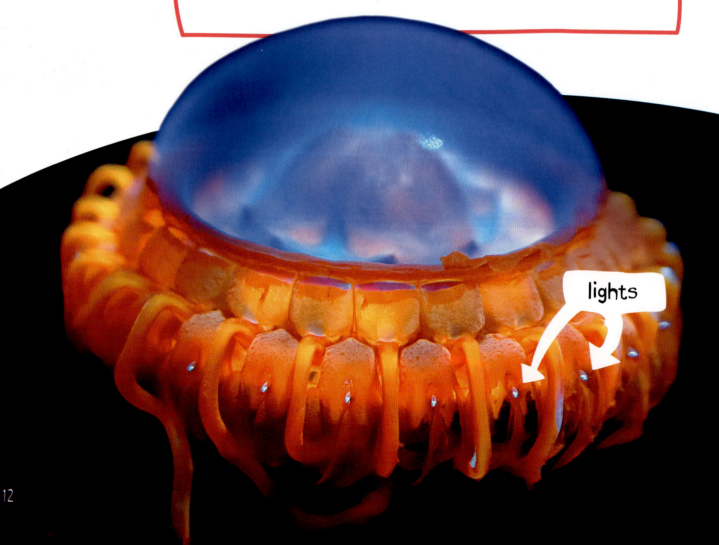

lights

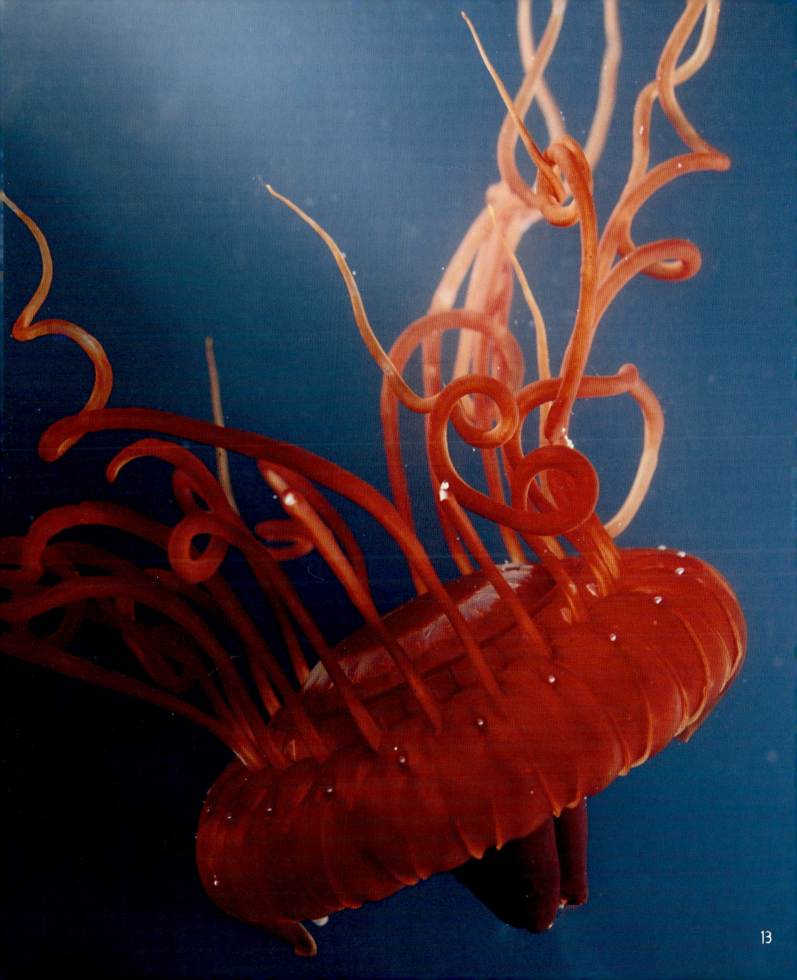

FIREFLY

Fireflies live in warm, moist areas. They can be found in forests and near rivers, ponds and lakes. A firefly begins its life as an egg. A larva hatches from the egg. Both a larva and an adult firefly can light up. As an adult, a firefly uses its flashing light to attract a mate. The light also warns predators to stay away. A firefly's blood is poisonous to some animals.

firefly larva

:: FUN FACT ::

Fireflies are in the larval stage for about one year. They eat worms and slugs.

RED TIDE

Red tides are blooms of very small bioluminescent plants. They are found in the world's oceans. Warm water, calm waters or low amounts of salt can cause the blooms. When a bloom happens, the ocean's surface looks reddish brown during the day. At night, the tiny plants give off a bright blue light. Ocean currents, ships and wind can churn up the water and spread red tides.

CLICK BEETLE

Click beetles are found all over the world. They are one of 200 types of bioluminescent beetles. Click beetles can give off blue and green light. Some use light to attract prey. Others use the light to attract a mate.

:: FUN FACT ::

Click beetles "play dead" to confuse predators. They can pretend to be dead for hours until the danger is gone.

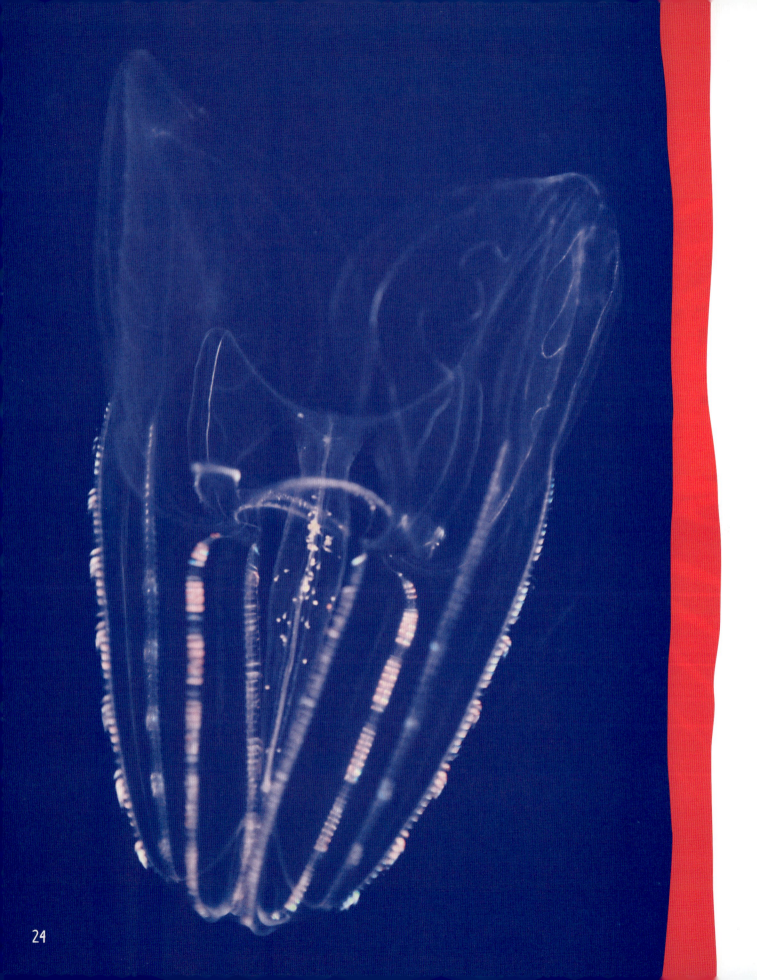

MIDWATER JELLYFISH

Midwater jellyfish are found at ocean depths of about 915 to 1,005 metres (3,000 to 3,300 feet). They have 32 tentacles. When bothered, this jellyfish lights up its waving tentacles. Sometimes its tentacles even fall off! Predators are confused by this and may swim away. The jellyfish's tentacles grow back later.

Under white light, the shortnose greeneye fish looks just like any other fish. But under UV light, its eyes and body light up green!

SHORTNOSE GREENEYE FISH

The shortnose greeneye fish is fluorescent. These fish absorb sunlight from the ocean's surface. Special eye lenses allow them to give off green light. The lenses also help them to see prey. Shortnose greeneye fish live in ocean depths of about 50 to 1,000 metres (164 to 3,280 feet).

GLOSSARY

ABSORB take in and hold

BIOLUMINESCENT able to make light as a living thing; certain animals, such as fireflies and deep-sea fish, are bioluminscent

BLOOM grow rapidly

CHURN move roughly

CURRENT movement of water in an ocean

FLUORESCENT giving out a bright light by using a certain type of energy; a fluorescent light turns light that people cannot see into a light that people can see

HATCH break out of an egg

LARVA animal at the stage of development between an egg and an adult

LURE attract something

MATE male or female partner of a pair of animals

POISON substance that can kill or harm someone

PREY animal hunted by another animal for food

SILK thin but strong thread made by an insect

TENTACLE long, flexible limb (such as a leg or an arm), used for moving, feeling and grabbing

UV LIGHT rays of light that cannot be seen by the human eye

BOOKS

Adaptation and Survival (Life Science Stories),
Louise and Richard Spilsbury (Raintree, 2017)

Animal (Eyewitness), DK (DK Children, 2015)

Deep Sea Anglerfish and other Fearsome Fish
(Creatures of the Deep), Rachel Lynette (Raintree, 2011)

WEBSITES

www.bbc.co.uk/nature/life/Lampyris_noctiluca
Watch videos and learn more about glow-worms.

www.dkfindout.com/uk/animals-and-nature/nocturnal-animals/glowing-in-dark/
See a close-up of a glowing firefly and learn more fun facts about animals that glow in the dark.

Comprehension QUESTIONS

1. Where do anglerfish live?

2. The South American polka dot tree frog and shortnose greeneye fish are both fluorescent. What does fluorescent mean? Hint: Use the glossary for help!

3. Which animal in this book is your favourite? Why?

::INDEX::

Antarctic Ocean 15

Atlantic Ocean 10, 15

caves 8

colours 6, 10, 12, 19, 20, 26, 28, 29

Gulf of Mexico 10, 22

larvae 16

mates 10, 15, 16, 20

ocean depths 12, 25, 29

plants 19

predators 6, 12, 16, 20, 22, 25

prey 10, 15, 20, 29

size 10, 22

sunlight 6, 26, 29

teeth 10, 15

UV light 26, 28